To the person who inspired me

<u>My Running Jou</u>

This running journal belongs to:

_____

Address:

_____

_____

_____

_____

Number: _____

Email: _____

Emergency Contacts:

_____   _____

_____   _____

_____   _____

_____   _____

My Running Journal
Copyright © Chris Allton, 2021
First published by Chris Allton 2021 via Amazon Kindle Direct Publishing
www.chrisallton.co.uk
ISBN - 9798702023533
Front cover design © 2021 by Chris Allton

Let's Get Physical

Here starts your journal for your ten-week running programme to getting healthier. Whether you are new to running, or you regularly complete marathons this journal will track your progress and let you clearly see your progress.

Start off by taking all your measurements so you can track them weekly and see your results. Set goals to achieve as you progress each week and form new habits over the ten-week period.

Then you move to the weekly plan and after each of these are your seven day plans noting diet, positive affirmations, motivational quotes and a chart to track specifically the exercise you do.

Whether you run every day, a few times a week or supplement your training with weight training or another type of exercise class, there is space to note your achievements. (If you don't do these extra activities and focus on running alone just leave those sections blank).

Measurements

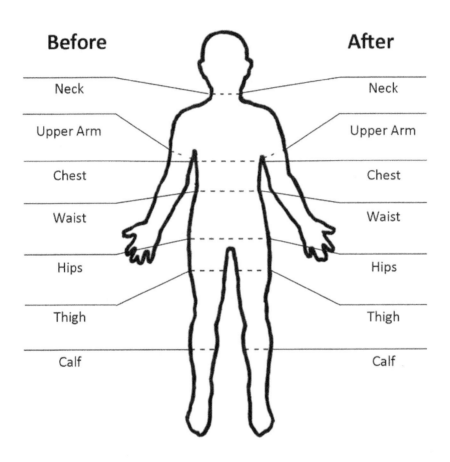

Before		After
Neck		Neck
Upper Arm		Upper Arm
Chest		Chest
Waist		Waist
Hips		Hips
Thigh		Thigh
Calf		Calf

As you start your 10-week journey, you need to see the progress you make. Progress (no matter how small) will encourage you even further. Remember, think what your final goal is and split that into ten weeks. Don't be too disheartened if you don't make huge progress all the time. It is the overall progress that matters.

	Wk. 1	Wk. 2	Wk. 3	Wk. 4	Wk. 5	Wk. 6	Wk. 7	Wk. 8	Wk. 9	Wk. 10	Change
Weight											
Bodyfat %											
Neck											
Arm											
Chest											
Waist											
Hips											
Thigh											
Calf											

My 10 Week Goals

Goal #1		Deadline
Plan		
Progress		

Goal #2		Deadline
Plan		
Progress		

Goal #3		Deadline
Plan		
Progress		

Goal #4		Deadline
Plan		
Progress		

Goal #5		Deadline
Plan		
Progress		

Goal #6		Deadline
Plan		
Progress		

Goal #7		Deadline
Plan		
Progress		

Goal #8		Deadline
Plan		
Progress		

Goal #9		Deadline
Plan		
Progress		

Goal #10		Deadline
Plan		
Progress		

Habit Tracker

It takes on average sixty-six days to form a new habit. So that is about nine and a half weeks, which is close enough to ten for arguments sake.

On the following pages are three habit trackers. For three new habits. These may link to your running routine (i.e., picking a time to do a run) or it could be something completely different. It may be some form of relaxation, or a mindful activity. It really is up to you. Cross off each day as you pass it.

Keeping the habit for ten weeks is not necessarily an easy task. Think long term and start small; set goals that have true value to you, not something that wastes your time; create a positive affirmation, to say each morning to remind yourself; find others with similar habits, set up a successful environment and visualize your goal. Remember repetition is the key. That's what makes it a habit.

70 Days to Form a New Habit

My new habit is _____

Week 1	1	2	3	4	5	6	7
Week 2	8	9	10	11	12	13	14
Week 3	15	16	17	18	19	20	21
Week 4	22	23	24	25	26	27	28
Week 5	29	30	31	32	33	34	35
Week 6	36	37	38	39	40	41	42
Week 7	43	44	45	46	47	48	49
Week 8	50	51	52	53	54	55	56
Week 9	57	58	59	60	61	62	63
Week 10	64	65	66	67	68	69	70

Well done, you've cracked it!

70 Days to Form a New Habit

My new habit is _____

Week 1	1	2	3	4	5	6	7
Week 2	8	9	10	11	12	13	14
Week 3	15	16	17	18	19	20	21
Week 4	22	23	24	25	26	27	28
Week 5	29	30	31	32	33	34	35
Week 6	36	37	38	39	40	41	42
Week 7	43	44	45	46	47	48	49
Week 8	50	51	52	53	54	55	56
Week 9	57	58	59	60	61	62	63
Week 10	64	65	66	67	68	69	70

Well done, you've cracked it!

70 Days to Form a New Habit

My new habit is _____

Week 1	1	2	3	4	5	6	7
Week 2	8	9	10	11	12	13	14
Week 3	15	16	17	18	19	20	21
Week 4	22	23	24	25	26	27	28
Week 5	29	30	31	32	33	34	35
Week 6	36	37	38	39	40	41	42
Week 7	43	44	45	46	47	48	49
Week 8	50	51	52	53	54	55	56
Week 9	57	58	59	60	61	62	63
Week 10	64	65	66	67	68	69	70

Well done, you've cracked it!

This Week's Goals

Factor	Current	Goal
Distance		
Weight		
Body Fat		
Other		

Workout	Nutrition

Other	Reward

Any new habits to develop?

Any old habits to ditch?

Day:	Date:

Today I am grateful for:

My positive thought for the day is:

"In two weeks, you'll feel it. In four weeks, you'll see it. In eight weeks, you'll hear it."

Breakfast	Lunch

Dinner	Snacks

Water	1	2	3	4	5	6	7	8	9	10	11	12	13	14	15

Sleep Time

     Bed – _____

     Awake – _____

     Total – _____

Supplements

Rating	1	2	3	4	5

What will I make better tomorrow?

Name of Run:		
Start:	Stop:	Total:

Warm up	
Run	Time	Distance	Calories

Route

Weight training						
Weight training						
Cool Down						

Class	Time	Calories

Notes	Total Time	Total Calories
	Rate Your Workout	Nailed it
		Spot on
		Average
		Meh
		OOOPS

Day:	Date:

Today I am grateful for:

My positive thought for the day is:

"Motivation is what gets you started. Habit is what keeps you going."

Breakfast	Lunch
Dinner	Snacks

Water	1	2	3	4	5	6	7	8	9	10	11	12	13	14	15

Sleep Time

Bed – _____

Awake – _____

Total – _____

Supplements

Rating	1	2	3	4	5

What will I make better tomorrow?

Name of Run:		

Start:	Stop:	Total:

Warm up				
Run		Time	Distance	Calories

Route

	Class		Time		Calories	
Weight training						
Weight training						
Cool Down						

Class	Time	Calories

Notes	Total Time	Total Calories
	Rate Your Workout	Nailed it
		Spot on
		Average
		Meh
		OOOPS

Day:	Date:

Today I am grateful for:

My positive thought for the day is:

"Sore today. Strong tomorrow."

Breakfast	Lunch
Dinner	Snacks

Water	1	2	3	4	5	6	7	8	9	10	11	12	13	14	15

Sleep Time

Bed – _____

Awake – _____

Total – _____

Supplements

Rating	1	2	3	4	5

What will I make better tomorrow?

Name of Run:			
Start:	Stop:	Total:	

Warm up				
Run	Time	Distance	Calories	

Route

Weight training						
Weight training						
Cool Down						

Class	Time	Calories

Notes	Total Time	Total Calories
	Rate Your Workout	Nailed it
		Spot on
		Average
		Meh
		OOOPS

Day:	Date:

Today I am grateful for:

My positive thought for the day is:

"It hurts now, but one day it will be your warmup."

Breakfast	Lunch
Dinner	Snacks

Water	1	2	3	4	5	6	7	8	9	10	11	12	13	14	15

Sleep Time	Supplements
Bed – _____	
Awake – _____	
Total – _____	

Rating	1	2	3	4	5

What will I make better tomorrow?

Name of Run:			
Start:	Stop:		Total:

Warm up				
Run		Time	Distance	Calories

Route

Weight training						
Weight training						
Cool Down						

Class	Time	Calories

Notes	Total Time	Total Calories
	Rate Your Workout	Nailed it	
		Spot on	
		Average	
		Meh	
		OOOPS	

Day:	Date:

Today I am grateful for:

My positive thought for the day is:

"When you feel like stopping, think about why you started."

Breakfast	Lunch
Dinner	Snacks

Water	1	2	3	4	5	6	7	8	9	10	11	12	13	14	15

Sleep Time	Supplements
Bed – _____	
Awake – _____	
Total – _____	

Rating	1	2	3	4	5

What will I make better tomorrow?

Name of Run:			
Start:	Stop:		Total:

Warm up			
Run		Time	Distance	Calories

Route

Weight training							
Weight training							
Cool Down							

Class	Time	Calories

Notes	Total Time	Total Calories
	Rate Your Workout	Nailed it	
		Spot on	
		Average	
		Meh	
		OOOPS	

Day:	Date:

Today I am grateful for:

My positive thought for the day is:

"Exercise is a celebration of what your body can do. Not a punishment for what you ate."

Breakfast	Lunch
Dinner	Snacks

Water	1	2	3	4	5	6	7	8	9	10	11	12	13	14	15

Sleep Time	Supplements
Bed – _____	
Awake – _____	
Total – _____	

Rating	1	2	3	4	5

What will I make better tomorrow?

Name of Run:		
Start:	Stop:	Total:

Warm up				
Run		Time	Distance	Calories

Route

Weight training						
Weight training						
Cool Down						

Class	Time	Calories

Notes	Total Time	Total Calories
	Rate Your Workout	Nailed it
		Spot on
		Average
		Meh
		OOOPS

Day:	Date:

Today I am grateful for:

My positive thought for the day is:

"Work out. Eat well. Be patient. Your body will reward you."

Breakfast	Lunch
Dinner	Snacks

Water	1	2	3	4	5	6	7	8	9	10	11	12	13	14	15

Sleep Time	Supplements
Bed – _____	
Awake – _____	
Total – _____	

Rating	1	2	3	4	5

What will I make better tomorrow?

Name of Run:		
Start:	Stop:	Total:

Warm up				
Run		Time	Distance	Calories

Route

Weight training							
Weight training							
Cool Down							

Class	Time	Calories

Notes	Total Time	Total Calories
	Rate Your Workout	Nailed it	
		Spot on	
		Average	
		Meh	
		OOOPS	

This Week's Goals

Factor	Current	Goal
Distance		
Weight		
Body Fat		
Other		

Workout

Nutrition

Other

Reward

Any new habits to develop?

Any old habits to ditch?

Day:	Date:

Today I am grateful for:

My positive thought for the day is:

"I will beat her. I will train harder. I will eat cleaner. I know her weaknesses. I know her strengths. She is the old me."

Breakfast	Lunch

Dinner	Snacks

Water	1	2	3	4	5	6	7	8	9	10	11	12	13	14	15

Sleep Time	Supplements
Bed – _____	
Awake – _____	
Total – _____	

Rating	1	2	3	4	5

What will I make better tomorrow?

Name of Run:			
Start:	Stop:		Total:

Warm up			
Run	Time	Distance	Calories

Route

Weight training						
Weight training						
Cool Down						

Class	Time	Calories

Notes	Total Time	Total Calories
	Rate Your Workout	Nailed it	
		Spot on	
		Average	
		Meh	
		OOOPS	

Day:	Date:

Today I am grateful for:

My positive thought for the day is:

"When you think about quitting, think about why you started."

Breakfast	Lunch
Dinner	Snacks

Water	1	2	3	4	5	6	7	8	9	10	11	12	13	14	15

Sleep Time

Bed – _____

Awake – _____

Total – _____

Supplements

Rating	1	2	3	4	5

What will I make better tomorrow?

Name of Run:		
Start:	Stop:	Total:

Warm up			
Run	Time	Distance	Calories

Route

Weight training	Weight	Width	Weight	Width	Weight	Width
	Rep	Rep	Rep	Rep	Rep	Rep
Weight training	Weight	Width	Weight	Width	Weight	Width
	Rep	Rep	Rep	Rep	Rep	Rep
Cool Down						

Class	Time	Calories

Notes	Total Time	Total Calories
	Rate Your Workout	Nailed it	
		Spot on	
		Average	
		Meh	
		OOOPS	

Day:	Date:

Today I am grateful for:

My positive thought for the day is:

"Your body can do it. It's time to convince your mind."

Breakfast	Lunch
Dinner	Snacks

Water	1	2	3	4	5	6	7	8	9	10	11	12	13	14	15

Sleep Time	Supplements
Bed – _____	
Awake – _____	
Total – _____	

Rating	1	2	3	4	5

What will I make better tomorrow?

Name of Run:			
Start:	Stop:	Total:	

Warm up				
Run		Time	Distance	Calories

Route

Weight training							
Weight training							
Cool Down							

Class	Time	Calories

Notes	Total Time	Total Calories
	Rate Your Workout	Nailed it
		Spot on
		Average
		Meh
		OOOPS

Day:	Date:

Today I am grateful for:

My positive thought for the day is:

"You get what you work for."

Breakfast	Lunch
Dinner	Snacks

Water	1	2	3	4	5	6	7	8	9	10	11	12	13	14	15

Sleep Time	Supplements
Bed – _____	
Awake – _____	
Total – _____	

Rating	1	2	3	4	5

What will I make better tomorrow?

Name of Run:			
Start:	Stop:		Total:

Warm up			
Run	Time	Distance	Calories

Route

Weight training						
Weight training						
Cool Down						

Class	Time	Calories

Notes	Total Time	Total Calories
	Rate Your Workout	Nailed it
		Spot on
		Average
		Meh
		OOOPS

Day:	Date:

Today I am grateful for:

My positive thought for the day is:

"You are stronger than you think."

Breakfast	Lunch

Dinner	Snacks

| Water | 1 | 2 | 3 | 4 | 5 | 6 | 7 | 8 | 9 | 10 | 11 | 12 | 13 | 14 | 15 |

Sleep Time

    Bed – _____

    Awake – _____

    Total – _____

Supplements

| Rating | 1 | 2 | 3 | 4 | 5 |

What will I make better tomorrow?

Name of Run:		

Start:	Stop:	Total:

Warm up	

Run		Time	Distance	Calories

Route

Weight training		Weight	Weight	Weight	Weight	Weight	Weight
Weight training		Reps Weight	Reps Weight	Reps Weight	Reps Weight	Reps Weight	Reps Weight
		Reps	Reps	Reps	Reps	Reps	Reps

Cool Down	

Class	Time	Calories

Notes	Total Time	Total Calories
	Rate Your Workout	Nailed it
		Spot on
		Average
		Meh
		OOOPS

Day:	Date:

Today I am grateful for:

My positive thought for the day is:

"May the next few months be a period of magnificent transformation."

Breakfast	Lunch
Dinner	Snacks

Water															

Sleep Time	Supplements
Bed – _____	
Awake – _____	
Total – _____	

Rating					

What will I make better tomorrow?

Name of Run:		
Start:	Stop:	Total:

Warm up				
Run		Time	Distance	Calories

Route

Weight training						
Weight training						
Cool Down						

Class	Time	Calories

Notes	Total Time	Total Calories	
	Rate Your Workout	Nailed it	
		Spot on	
		Average	
		Meh	
		OOOPS	

Day:	Date:

Today I am grateful for:

My positive thought for the day is:

"No matter how slow you go, you're still lapping everybody on the couch."

Breakfast	Lunch
Dinner	Snacks

Water	1	2	3	4	5	6	7	8	9	10	11	12	13	14	15

Sleep Time	Supplements
Bed – _____	
Awake – _____	
Total – _____	

Rating	1	2	3	4	5

What will I make better tomorrow?

Name of Run:		

Start:	Stop:	Total:

Warm up				
Run		Time	Distance	Calories

Route

Weight training		Weight	Weight	Weight	Weight	Weight	Weight
		Rep	Rep	Rep	Rep	Rep	Rep
Weight training							
		Rep	Rep	Rep	Rep	Rep	Rep
Cool Down							

Class	Time	Calories

Notes	Total Time	Total Calories
	Rate Your Workout	Nailed it	
		Spot on	
		Average	
		Meh	
		OOOPS	

This Week's Goals

Factor	Current	Goal
Distance		
Weight		
Body Fat		
Other		

Workout	Nutrition

Other	Reward

Any new habits to develop?

Any old habits to ditch?

Day:	Date:

Today I am grateful for:

My positive thought for the day is:

"Your legs are not giving out. Your head is giving up. Keep going."

Breakfast	Lunch

Dinner	Snacks

Water	1	2	3	4	5	6	7	8	9	10	11	12	13	14	15

Sleep Time

Bed – _____

Awake – _____

Total – _____

Supplements

Rating	1	2	3	4	5

What will I make better tomorrow?

Name of Run:		
Start:	Stop:	Total:

Warm up		
Run	Time	Distance	Calories

Route

Weight training						
Weight training						
Cool Down						

Class	Time	Calories

Notes	Total Time	Total Calories
	Rate Your Workout	Nailed it
		Spot on
		Average
		Meh
		OOOPS

Day:	Date:

Today I am grateful for:

My positive thought for the day is:

"You're far too smart to be the only thing standing in your way."

Breakfast	Lunch
Dinner	Snacks

Water	1	2	3	4	5	6	7	8	9	10	11	12	13	14	15

Sleep Time

Bed – _____

Awake – _____

Total – _____

Supplements

Rating	1	2	3	4	5

What will I make better tomorrow?

Name of Run:			
Start:	Stop:		Total:

Warm up			
Run		Time	Distance	Calories

Route

Weight training								
Weight training								
Cool Down								

Class	Time	Calories

Notes	Total Time	Total Calories
	Rate Your Workout	Nailed it
		Spot on
		Average
		Meh
		OOOPS

Day:	Date:

Today I am grateful for:

My positive thought for the day is:

"If you can't stop thinking about it, don't stop working for it."

Breakfast	Lunch
Dinner	Snacks

Water	1	2	3	4	5	6	7	8	9	10	11	12	13	14	15

Sleep Time	Supplements
Bed – _____	
Awake – _____	
Total – _____	

Rating	1	2	3	4	5

What will I make better tomorrow?

Name of Run:		

Start:	Stop:	Total:

Warm up				
Run		Time	Distance	Calories

Route

Weight training						
Weight training						
Cool Down						

Class	Time	Calories

Notes	Total Time	Total Calories
	Rate Your Workout	Nailed it
		Spot on
		Average
		Meh
		OOOPS

Day:	Date:

Today I am grateful for:

My positive thought for the day is:

"I go to the gym because I think my great personality could use a banging body."

Breakfast	Lunch
Dinner	Snacks

Water	1	2	3	4	5	6	7	8	9	10	11	12	13	14	15

Sleep Time	Supplements
Bed – _____	
Awake – _____	
Total – _____	

Rating	1	2	3	4	5

What will I make better tomorrow?

Name of Run:		
Start:	Stop:	Total:

Warm up				
Run		Time	Distance	Calories

Route

Weight training					
Weight training					
Cool Down					

Class	Time	Calories

Notes	Total Time	Total Calories
	Rate Your Workout	Nailed it
		Spot on
		Average
		Meh
		OOOPS

Day:	Date:

Today I am grateful for:

My positive thought for the day is:

"No pain. No gain. Shut up and train."

Breakfast	Lunch
Dinner	Snacks

Water	1	2	3	4	5	6	7	8	9	10	11	12	13	14	15

Sleep Time

Bed – _____

Awake – _____

Total – _____

Supplements

Rating	1	2	3	4	5

What will I make better tomorrow?

Name of Run:		
Start:	Stop:	Total:

Warm up				
Run		Time	Distance	Calories

Route

Weight training							
Weight training							
Cool Down							

Class	Time	Calories

Notes	Total Time	Total Calories
	Rate Your Workout	Nailed it
		Spot on
		Average
		Meh
		OOOPS

Day:	Date:

Today I am grateful for:

My positive thought for the day is:

"I never regret it when I do it, but I always regret it when I don't."

Breakfast	Lunch
Dinner	Snacks

Water	1	2	3	4	5	6	7	8	9	10	11	12	13	14	15

Sleep Time	Supplements
Bed – _____	
Awake – _____	
Total – _____	

Rating	1	2	3	4	5

What will I make better tomorrow?

Name of Run:		
Start:	Stop:	Total:

Warm up				
Run	Time	Distance	Calories	
Route				
Weight training	Weight	Range	Watts	Length	Knots	Weight
Weight training	Weight	Range	Watts	Length	Knots	Weight
Cool Down						

Class	Time	Calories

Notes	Total Time	Total Calories
	Rate Your Workout	Nailed it	
		Spot on	
		Average	
		Meh	
		OOOPS	

Day:	Date:

Today I am grateful for:

My positive thought for the day is:

"It always seems impossible until its done." — Nelson Mandela

Breakfast	Lunch

Dinner	Snacks

| Water | 1 | 2 | 3 | 4 | 5 | 6 | 7 | 8 | 9 | 10 | 11 | 12 | 13 | 14 | 15 |

Sleep Time   Supplements

      Bed – _____

      Awake – _____

      Total – _____

| Rating | 1 | 2 | 3 | 4 | 5 |

What will I make better tomorrow?

Name of Run:			
Start:	Stop:		Total:

Warm up			
Run	Time	Distance	Calories

Route

Weight training						
Weight training						
Cool Down						

Class	Time	Calories

Notes	Total Time	Total Calories
	Rate Your Workout	Nailed it
		Spot on
		Average
		Meh
		OOOPS

This Week's Goals

Factor	Current	Goal
Distance		
Weight		
Body Fat		
Other		

Workout	Nutrition
Other	Reward

Any new habits to develop?

Any old habits to ditch?

Day:	Date:

Today I am grateful for:

My positive thought for the day is:

"Note to Self: You gotta do this for you. This is for you. This isn't about anybody. Live for you. Honor you. Never lose sight of that."

Breakfast	Lunch
Dinner	Snacks

Water	1	2	3	4	5	6	7	8	9	10	11	12	13	14	15

Sleep Time	Supplements

Bed – _____

Awake – _____

Total – _____

Rating	1	2	3	4	5

What will I make better tomorrow?

Name of Run:		
Start:	Stop:	Total:

Warm up				
Run		Time	Distance	Calories

Route

Weight training	Weight	Weight	Weight	Reps	Weight	Reps
Weight training	Reps	Weight	Reps	Reps	Reps	Reps
Cool Down						

Class	Time	Calories

Notes	Total Time	Total Calories
	Rate Your Workout	Nailed it
		Spot on
		Average
		Meh
		OOOPS

Day:	Date:

Today I am grateful for:

My positive thought for the day is:

"Wish less. Work more."

Breakfast	Lunch

Dinner	Snacks

Water	1	2	3	4	5	6	7	8	9	10	11	12	13	14	15

Sleep Time

      Bed – _____

      Awake – _____

      Total – _____

Supplements

Rating	1	2	3	4	5

What will I make better tomorrow?

Name of Run:		
Start:	Stop:	Total:

Warm up				
Run		Time	Distance	Calories

Route

Weight training		Weight	Weight	Weight	Weight	Weight	Weight
		Rep	Rep	Rep	Rep	Rep	Rep
Weight training							
		Rep	Rep	Rep	Rep	Rep	Rep
Cool Down							

Class	Time	Calories

Notes	Total Time	Total Calories	
	Rate Your Workout	Nailed it	
		Spot on	
		Average	
		Meh	
		OOOPS	

Day:	Date:

Today I am grateful for:

My positive thought for the day is:

"If it doesn't challenge you It doesn't change you."

Breakfast	Lunch
Dinner	Snacks

Water	1	2	3	4	5	6	7	8	9	10	11	12	13	14	15

Sleep Time

Bed – _____

Awake – _____

Total – _____

Supplements

Rating	1	2	3	4	5

What will I make better tomorrow?

Name of Run:		
Start:	Stop:	Total:

Warm up				
Run		Time	Distance	Calories

Route

Weight training						
Weight training						
Cool Down						

Class	Time	Calories

Notes	Total Time	Total Calories
	Rate Your Workout	Nailed it	
		Spot on	
		Average	
		Meh	
		OOOPS	

Day:	Date:

Today I am grateful for:

My positive thought for the day is:

"When a girl is working out and tightens her ponytail, you know it's about to go down."

Breakfast	Lunch

Dinner	Snacks

Water | | | | | | | | | | | | | | |

Sleep Time	Supplements
Bed – _____	
Awake – _____	
Total – _____	

Rating | | | | | |

What will I make better tomorrow?

Name of Run:		

Start:	Stop:	Total:

Warm up	

Run		Time	Distance	Calories

Route

Weight training								

Cool Down	

	Class	Time	Calories

Notes	Total Time	Total Calories

	Rate Your Workout	Nailed it	
		Spot on	
		Average	
		Meh	
		OOOPS	

Day:	Date:

Today I am grateful for:

My positive thought for the day is:

"I already know what giving up feels like. I want to see what happens if I don't." — Neila Rey

Breakfast	Lunch
Dinner	Snacks

Water	1	2	3	4	5	6	7	8	9	10	11	12	13	14	15

Sleep Time	Supplements
Bed – _____	
Awake – _____	
Total – _____	

Rating	1	2	3	4	5

What will I make better tomorrow?

Name of Run:		
Start:	Stop:	Total:

Warm up	

Run		Time	Distance	Calories

Route

Weight training		Weight	Weight	Weight	Weight	Weight	Weight
		Reps	Reps	Reps	Reps	Reps	Reps
Weight training		Weight	Weight	Weight	Weight	Weight	Weight
		Reps	Reps	Reps	Reps	Reps	Reps
Cool Down							

Class	Time	Calories

Notes	Total Time	Total Calories
	Rate Your Workout	Nailed it	
		Spot on	
		Average	
		Meh	
		OOOPS	

Day:	Date:

Today I am grateful for:

My positive thought for the day is:

"At first they'll ask why you're doing it. Later, they'll ask how you did it."

Breakfast	Lunch
Dinner	Snacks

Water	1	2	3	4	5	6	7	8	9	10	11	12	13	14	15

Sleep Time	Supplements
Bed – _____	
Awake – _____	
Total – _____	

Rating	1	2	3	4	5

What will I make better tomorrow?

Name of Run:		
Start:	Stop:	Total:

Warm up	
Run	

	Time	Distance	Calories

Route

Weight training							
Weight training							

Cool Down	

Class	Time	Calories

Notes	Total Time	Total Calories
	Rate Your Workout	Nailed it	
		Spot on	
		Average	
		Meh	
		OOOPS	

Day:	Date:

Today I am grateful for:

My positive thought for the day is:

"A 30-minute workout is just two percent of your day. No excuses."

Breakfast	Lunch
Dinner	Snacks

Water	1	2	3	4	5	6	7	8	9	10	11	12	13	14	15

Sleep Time	Supplements
Bed – _____	
Awake – _____	
Total – _____	

Rating	1	2	3	4	5

What will I make better tomorrow?

Name of Run:		

Start:	Stop:	Total:

Warm up	

Run	Time	Distance	Calories

Route

Weight training	Reps	Weight	Weight	Weight	Weight	Weight
Weight training	Reps	Reps	Reps	Reps	Reps	Reps
Cool Down						

Class	Time	Calories

Notes	Total Time	Total Calories
	Rate Your Workout	Nailed it	
		Spot on	
		Average	
		Meh	
		OOOPS	

This Week's Goals

Factor	Current	Goal
Distance		
Weight		
Body Fat		
Other		

Workout	Nutrition

Other	Reward

Any new habits to develop?

Any old habits to ditch?

Day:	Date:

Today I am grateful for:

My positive thought for the day is:

"Sore. The most satisfying pain."

Breakfast	Lunch

Dinner	Snacks

Water	1	2	3	4	5	6	7	8	9	10	11	12	13	14	15

Sleep Time

    Bed – _____

    Awake – _____

    Total – _____

Supplements

Rating	1	2	3	4	5

What will I make better tomorrow?

Name of Run:		
Start:	Stop:	Total:

Warm up		
Run	Time	Distance	Calories

Route

Weight training						
Weight training						
Cool Down		

Class	Time	Calories

Notes	Total Time	Total Calories
	Rate Your Workout	Nailed it	
		Spot on	
		Average	
		Meh	
		OOOPS	

Day:	Date:

Today I am grateful for:

My positive thought for the day is:

"Your mind will quit 100 times before your body ever does. Feel the pain and do it anyway."

Breakfast	Lunch
Dinner	Snacks

Water	1	2	3	4	5	6	7	8	9	10	11	12	13	14	15

Sleep Time

       Bed – _____

       Awake – _____

       Total – _____

Supplements

Rating	1	2	3	4	5

What will I make better tomorrow?

Name of Run:		
Start:	Stop:	Total:

Warm up			
Run	Time	Distance	Calories

Route

Weight training						
Weight training						
Cool Down						

Class	Time	Calories

Notes	Total Time	Total Calories	
	Rate Your Workout	Nailed it	
		Spot on	
		Average	
		Meh	
		OOOPS	

Day:	Date:

Today I am grateful for:

My positive thought for the day is:

"BLABLABLA. Go workout."

Breakfast	Lunch
Dinner	Snacks

Water	1	2	3	4	5	6	7	8	9	10	11	12	13	14	15

Sleep Time	Supplements
Bed – _____	
Awake – _____	
Total – _____	

Rating	1	2	3	4	5

What will I make better tomorrow?

Name of Run:			

Start:	Stop:	Total:

Warm up			
Run	Time	Distance	Calories

Route

Weight training						
Weight training						
Cool Down						

Class	Time	Calories

Notes	Total Time	Total Calories
	Rate Your Workout	Nailed it
		Spot on
		Average
		Meh
		OOOPS

Day:	Date:

Today I am grateful for:

My positive thought for the day is:

"I'm not trying to look perfect. I just want to feel better, look great, know I'm healthy, and rock any outfit I choose."

Breakfast	Lunch
Dinner	Snacks

Water	1	2	3	4	5	6	7	8	9	10	11	12	13	14	15

Sleep Time	Supplements
Bed – _____	
Awake – _____	
Total – _____	

Rating	1	2	3	4	5

What will I make better tomorrow?

Name of Run:				
Start:	Stop:		Total:	

Warm up				
Run		Time	Distance	Calories

Route				

Weight training						
Weight training						
Cool Down						

Class	Time	Calories

Notes	Total Time	Total Calories	
	Rate Your Workout	Nailed it	
		Spot on	
		Average	
		Meh	
		OOOPS	

Day:	Date:

Today I am grateful for:

My positive thought for the day is:

"Success starts with self-discipline."

Breakfast	Lunch
Dinner	Snacks

Water	1	2	3	4	5	6	7	8	9	10	11	12	13	14	15

Sleep Time	Supplements
Bed – _____	
Awake – _____	
Total – _____	

Rating	1	2	3	4	5

What will I make better tomorrow?

Name of Run:		

Start:	Stop:	Total:

Warm up				
Run		Time	Distance	Calories

Route

Weight training					
Weight training					
Cool Down					

Class	Time	Calories

Notes	Total Time	Total Calories
	Rate Your Workout	Nailed it
		Spot on
		Average
		Meh
		OOOPS

Day:	Date:

Today I am grateful for:

My positive thought for the day is:

"Fall in love with taking care of your body."

Breakfast	Lunch
Dinner	Snacks

Water	1	2	3	4	5	6	7	8	9	10	11	12	13	14	15

Sleep Time	Supplements
Bed – _____	
Awake – _____	
Total – _____	

Rating	1	2	3	4	5

What will I make better tomorrow?

Name of Run:			
Start:	Stop:		Total:

Warm up			
Run		Time	Distance	Calories

Route

Weight training						
Weight training						
Cool Down						

Class	Time	Calories

Notes	Total Time	Total Calories
	Rate Your Workout	Nailed it
		Spot on
		Average
		Meh
		OOOPS

Day:	Date:

Today I am grateful for:

My positive thought for the day is:

"Self-confidence is a superpower. Once you start to believe in yourself, magic starts happening."

Breakfast	Lunch
Dinner	Snacks

Water	1	2	3	4	5	6	7	8	9	10	11	12	13	14	15

Sleep Time	Supplements
Bed – _____	
Awake – _____	
Total – _____	

Rating	1	2	3	4	5

What will I make better tomorrow?

Name of Run:		
Start:	Stop:	Total:

Warm up				
Run	Time	Distance	Calories	
Route				
Weight training				
Weight training				
Cool Down				

Class	Time	Calories

Notes	Total Time	Total Calories	
	Rate Your Workout	Nailed it	
		Spot on	
		Average	
		Meh	
		OOOPS	

This Week's Goals

Factor	Current	Goal
Distance		
Weight		
Body Fat		
Other		

Workout

Nutrition

Other

Reward

Any new habits to develop?

Any old habits to ditch?

Day:	Date:

Today I am grateful for:

My positive thought for the day is:

"Because the next few months will go by whether you work out or not. Make them count."

Breakfast	Lunch
Dinner	Snacks

Water	1	2	3	4	5	6	7	8	9	10	11	12	13	14	15

Sleep Time	Supplements
Bed – _____	
Awake – _____	
Total – _____	

Rating	1	2	3	4	5

What will I make better tomorrow?

Name of Run:			
Start:	Stop:		Total:

Warm up			
Run	Time	Distance	Calories

Route

Weight training	Weight	Weight	Weight	Weight	Weight	Weight
	Reps	Reps	Reps	Reps	Reps	Reps
Weight training	Weight	Weight	Weight	Weight	Weight	Weight
	Reps	Reps	Reps	Reps	Reps	Reps
Cool Down						

Class	Time	Calories

Notes	Total Time	Total Calories
	Rate Your Workout	Nailed it
		Spot on
		Average
		Meh
		OOOPS

Day:	Date:

Today I am grateful for:

My positive thought for the day is:

"If it burns, you're getting closer."

Breakfast	Lunch
Dinner	Snacks

Water	1	2	3	4	5	6	7	8	9	10	11	12	13	14	15

Sleep Time	Supplements
Bed – _____	
Awake – _____	
Total – _____	

Rating	1	2	3	4	5

What will I make better tomorrow?

Name of Run:			
Start:	Stop:		Total:

Warm up				
Run		Time	Distance	Calories

Route

Weight training	Reps	Weight	Weight	Set 1	Reps	Weight
Weight training						
Cool Down						

Class	Time	Calories

Notes	Total Time	Total Calories
	Rate Your Workout	Nailed it
		Spot on
		Average
		Meh
		OOOPS

Day:	Date:

Today I am grateful for:

My positive thought for the day is:

"Today, I ~~have to~~ get to work out."

Breakfast	Lunch
Dinner	Snacks

Water | 1 | 2 | 3 | 4 | 5 | 6 | 7 | 8 | 9 | 10 | 11 | 12 | 13 | 14 | 15 |

Sleep Time	Supplements
Bed – _____	
Awake – _____	
Total – _____	

Rating | 1 | 2 | 3 | 4 | 5 |

What will I make better tomorrow?

Name of Run:			

Start:	Stop:	Total:

Warm up			
Run	Time	Distance	Calories

Route

Weight training	Reps	Weight	Reps	Weight	Reps	Weight
Weight training	Reps	Weight	Reps	Weight	Reps	Weight
Cool Down	Reps	Reps	Reps	Reps	Reps	Reps

Class	Time	Calories

Notes	Total Time	Total Calories
	Rate Your Workout	Nailed it
		Spot on
		Average
		Meh
		OOOPS

Day:	Date:

Today I am grateful for:

My positive thought for the day is:

"Look in the mirror ... That's your competition."

Breakfast	Lunch
Dinner	Snacks

Water	1	2	3	4	5	6	7	8	9	10	11	12	13	14	15

Sleep Time	Supplements
Bed – _____	
Awake – _____	
Total – _____	

Rating	1	2	3	4	5

What will I make better tomorrow?

Name of Run:			

Start:	Stop:	Total:

Warm up	

Run		Time	Distance	Calories

Route

Weight training							
Weight training							
Cool Down							

Class	Time	Calories

Notes	Total Time	Total Calories
	Rate Your Workout	Nailed it	
		Spot on	
		Average	
		Meh	
		OOOPS	

Day:	Date:

Today I am grateful for:

My positive thought for the day is:

"Progress: you might not be where you want to be, but you're not where you used to be."

Breakfast	Lunch
Dinner	Snacks

Water	1	2	3	4	5	6	7	8	9	10	11	12	13	14	15

Sleep Time

Bed – _____

Awake – _____

Total – _____

Rating	1	2	3	4	5

Supplements

What will I make better tomorrow?

Name of Run:		

Start:	Stop:	Total:

Warm up				
Run		Time	Distance	Calories

Route

Weight training	Reps	Weight	Reps	Weight	Reps	Weight
Weight training	Reps	Weight	Reps	Weight	Reps	Weight
Cool Down						

Class	Time	Calories

Notes	Total Time	Total Calories
	Rate Your Workout	Nailed it
		Spot on
		Average
		Meh
		OOOPS

Day:	Date:

Today I am grateful for:

My positive thought for the day is:

"One workout at a time. One day at a time. One meal at a time."

Breakfast	Lunch
Dinner	Snacks

Water	1	2	3	4	5	6	7	8	9	10	11	12	13	14	15

Sleep Time

        Bed – _____

        Awake – _____

        Total – _____

Supplements

Rating	1	2	3	4	5

What will I make better tomorrow?

Name of Run:		
Start:	Stop:	Total:

Warm up				
Run		Time	Distance	Calories

Route

Weight training							
Weight training							
Cool Down							

Class	Time	Calories

Notes	Total Time	Total Calories
	Rate Your Workout	Nailed it	
		Spot on	
		Average	
		Meh	
		OOOPS	

Day:	Date:

Today I am grateful for:

My positive thought for the day is:

"Be stronger than your strongest excuse."

Breakfast	Lunch
Dinner	Snacks

Water	1	2	3	4	5	6	7	8	9	10	11	12	13	14	15

Sleep Time	Supplements

Bed – _____

Awake – _____

Total – _____

Rating	1	2	3	4	5

What will I make better tomorrow?

Name of Run:		
Start:	Stop:	Total:

Warm up				
Run		Time	Distance	Calories

Route

Weight training	Weight	Weight	Weight	Weight	Weight	Weight
Weight training	Reps Weight	Reps Weight	Reps Weight	Reps Weight	Reps Weight	Reps Weight
Cool Down						

Class	Time	Calories

Notes	Total Time	Total Calories
	Rate Your Workout	Nailed it
		Spot on
		Average
		Meh
		OOOPS

This Week's Goals

Factor	Current	Goal
Distance		
Weight		
Body Fat		
Other		

Workout	Nutrition

Other	Reward

Any new habits to develop?

Any old habits to ditch?

Day:	Date:

Today I am grateful for:

My positive thought for the day is:

"Hustle for that muscle."

Breakfast	Lunch
Dinner	**Snacks**

Water	1	2	3	4	5	6	7	8	9	10	11	12	13	14	15

Sleep Time   Supplements

       Bed – _____

       Awake – _____

       Total – _____

Rating	1	2	3	4	5

What will I make better tomorrow?

Name of Run:		
Start:	Stop:	Total:

Warm up				
Run		Time	Distance	Calories

Route

Weight training						
Weight training						
Cool Down						

Class	Time	Calories

Notes	Total Time	Total Calories
	Rate Your Workout	Nailed it	
		Spot on	
		Average	
		Meh	
		OOOPS	

Day:	Date:

Today I am grateful for:

My positive thought for the day is:

"Slow progress is better than no progress."

Breakfast	Lunch
Dinner	Snacks

Water	1	2	3	4	5	6	7	8	9	10	11	12	13	14	15

Sleep Time

Bed – _____

Awake – _____

Total – _____

Supplements

Rating	1	2	3	4	5

What will I make better tomorrow?

Name of Run:		

Start:	Stop:	Total:

Warm up	

Run	Time	Distance	Calories

Route

Weight training						
Weight training						
Cool Down						

Class	Time	Calories

Notes	Total Time	Total Calories
	Rate Your Workout	Nailed it	
		Spot on	
		Average	
		Meh	
		OOOPS	

Day:	Date:

Today I am grateful for:

My positive thought for the day is:

"Don't tell people your plans. Show them your results."

Breakfast	Lunch
Dinner	Snacks

Water	1	2	3	4	5	6	7	8	9	10	11	12	13	14	15

Sleep Time	Supplements
Bed – _____	
Awake – _____	
Total – _____	

Rating	1	2	3	4	5

What will I make better tomorrow?

Name of Run:						

Start:	Stop:	Total:

Warm up				
Run	Time	Distance	Calories	

Route

Weight training	Weight	Weight	Sets	Weight	Reps	Weight
Weight training	Weight	Weight	Reps	Reps	Reps	Reps

Cool Down	

Class	Time	Calories

Notes	Total Time	Total Calories
	Rate Your Workout	Nailed it	
		Spot on	
		Average	
		Meh	
		OOOPS	

Day:	Date:

Today I am grateful for:

My positive thought for the day is:

"My summer body is in progress."

Breakfast	Lunch
Dinner	Snacks

Water	1	2	3	4	5	6	7	8	9	10	11	12	13	14	15

Sleep Time

Bed – _____

Awake – _____

Total – _____

Supplements

Rating	1	2	3	4	5

What will I make better tomorrow?

Name of Run:		
Start:	Stop:	Total:

Warm up	

Run	Time	Distance	Calories

Route

Weight training							
Weight training							

Cool Down	

Class	Time	Calories

Notes	Total Time	Total Calories
	Rate Your Workout	Nailed it
		Spot on
		Average
		Meh
		OOOPS

Day:	Date:

Today I am grateful for:

My positive thought for the day is:

"Push yourself because no one else is going to do it for you."

Breakfast	Lunch
Dinner	Snacks

Water	1	2	3	4	5	6	7	8	9	10	11	12	13	14	15

Sleep Time	Supplements
Bed – _____	
Awake – _____	
Total – _____	

Rating	1	2	3	4	5

What will I make better tomorrow?

Name of Run:		
Start:	Stop:	Total:

Warm up				
Run		Time	Distance	Calories
Route				
Weight training						
Weight training						
Cool Down				

Class	Time	Calories

Notes	Total Time	Total Calories
	Rate Your Workout	Nailed it	
		Spot on	
		Average	
		Meh	
		OOOPS	

Day:	Date:

Today I am grateful for:

My positive thought for the day is:

"A little progress each day adds up to big results."

Breakfast	Lunch
Dinner	Snacks

Water	1	2	3	4	5	6	7	8	9	10	11	12	13	14	15

Sleep Time	Supplements
Bed – _____	
Awake – _____	
Total – _____	

Rating	1	2	3	4	5

What will I make better tomorrow?

Name of Run:		
Start:	Stop:	Total:

Warm up				
Run	Time	Distance	Calories	
Route				

Weight training						
Weight training						
Cool Down						

Class	Time	Calories

Notes	Total Time	Total Calories
	Rate Your Workout	Nailed it	
		Spot on	
		Average	
		Meh	
		OOOPS	

Day:	Date:

Today I am grateful for:

My positive thought for the day is:

"It comes down to one simple thing: How bad do you want it?"

Breakfast	Lunch
Dinner	Snacks

Water	1	2	3	4	5	6	7	8	9	10	11	12	13	14	15

Sleep Time	Supplements
Bed – _____	
Awake – _____	
Total – _____	

Rating	1	2	3	4	5

What will I make better tomorrow?

Name of Run:			
Start:	Stop:		Total:

Warm up			
Run	Time	Distance	Calories

Route

Weight training						
Weight training						
Cool Down						

Class	Time	Calories

Notes	Total Time	Total Calories
	Rate Your Workout	Nailed it
		Spot on
		Average
		Meh
		OOOPS

This Week's Goals

Factor	Current	Goal
Distance		
Weight		
Body Fat		
Other		

Workout

Nutrition

Other

Reward

Any new habits to develop?

Any old habits to ditch?

Day:	Date:

Today I am grateful for:

My positive thought for the day is:

"Believe in yourself and you will be unstoppable."

Breakfast	Lunch
Dinner	Snacks

Water	1	2	3	4	5	6	7	8	9	10	11	12	13	14	15

Sleep Time

      Bed – _____

      Awake – _____

      Total – _____

Supplements

Rating	1	2	3	4	5

What will I make better tomorrow?

Name of Run:		
Start:	Stop:	Total:

Warm up			
Run	Time	Distance	Calories

Route

Weight training	Weight	Weight	Weight	Weight	Weight	Weight
Weight training	Weight	Weight	Weight	Weight	Weight	Weight
Cool Down						

Class	Time	Calories

Notes	Total Time	Total Calories
	Rate Your Workout	Nailed it	
		Spot on	
		Average	
		Meh	
		OOOPS	

Day:	Date:

Today I am grateful for:

My positive thought for the day is:

"Good things come to those who sweat."

Breakfast	Lunch
Dinner	**Snacks**

Water	1	2	3	4	5	6	7	8	9	10	11	12	13	14	15

Sleep Time	Supplements
Bed – _____	
Awake – _____	
Total – _____	

Rating	1	2	3	4	5

What will I make better tomorrow?

Name of Run:			
Start:	Stop:		Total:

Warm up				
Run		Time	Distance	Calories

Route

Weight training	Reps	Weight	Reps	Weight	Reps	Weight
Weight training						
Cool Down						

Class	Time	Calories

Notes	Total Time	Total Calories
	Rate Your Workout	Nailed it
		Spot on
		Average
		Meh
		OOOPS

Day:	Date:

Today I am grateful for:

My positive thought for the day is:

"The reason I exercise is for the quality of life I enjoy." Kenneth H. Cooper

Breakfast	Lunch
Dinner	Snacks

Water	1	2	3	4	5	6	7	8	9	10	11	12	13	14	15

Sleep Time	Supplements
Bed – _____	
Awake – _____	
Total – _____	

Rating	1	2	3	4	5

What will I make better tomorrow?

Name of Run:		

Start:	Stop:	Total:

Warm up				
Run		Time	Distance	Calories

Route

Weight training							
Weight training							
Cool Down							

Class	Time	Calories

Notes	Total Time	Total Calories
	Rate Your Workout	Nailed it	
		Spot on	
		Average	
		Meh	
		OOOPS	

Day:	Date:

Today I am grateful for:

My positive thought for the day is:

"The only bad workout is the one that didn't happen."

Breakfast	Lunch
Dinner	Snacks

Water	1	2	3	4	5	6	7	8	9	10	11	12	13	14	15

Sleep Time

Bed – _____

Awake – _____

Total – _____

Supplements

Rating	1	2	3	4	5

What will I make better tomorrow?

Name of Run:		
Start:	Stop:	Total:

Warm up	
Run	Time	Distance	Calories

Route

Weight training		Weight	Weight	Weight	Weight	Weight	Weight
Weight training		Reps/Distance	Reps/Weight	Reps/Distance	Reps/Weight	Reps/Weight	Reps/Weight
Cool Down							

Class	Time	Calories

Notes	Total Time	Total Calories
	Rate Your Workout	Nailed it	
		Spot on	
		Average	
		Meh	
		OOOPS	

Day:	Date:

Today I am grateful for:

My positive thought for the day is:

"The pain you feel today will be the strength you feel tomorrow."

Breakfast	Lunch
Dinner	Snacks

Water	1	2	3	4	5	6	7	8	9	10	11	12	13	14	15

Sleep Time	Supplements
Bed – _____	
Awake – _____	
Total – _____	

Rating	1	2	3	4	5

What will I make better tomorrow?

Name of Run:				

Start:	Stop:		Total:	

Warm up				

Run		Time	Distance	Calories

Route

Weight training	Weight	Weight	Weight	Weight	Weight	Weight
	Reps	Reps	Reps	Reps	Reps	Reps
Weight training	Weight	Weight	Weight	Weight	Weight	Weight
	Reps	Reps	Reps	Reps	Reps	Reps

Cool Down	

Class	Time	Calories

Notes	Total Time	Total Calories
	Rate Your Workout	Nailed it	
		Spot on	
		Average	
		Meh	
		OOOPS	

Day:	Date:

Today I am grateful for:

My positive thought for the day is:

"For me, exercise is more than just physical – it's therapeutic."

Breakfast	Lunch
Dinner	Snacks

Water	1	2	3	4	5	6	7	8	9	10	11	12	13	14	15

Sleep Time

        Bed – _____

        Awake – _____

        Total – _____

Supplements

Rating	1	2	3	4	5

What will I make better tomorrow?

Name of Run:		
Start:	Stop:	Total:

		Time	Distance	Calories
Warm up				
Run				

Route

	Reps	Weight	Weight	Weight	Weight	Weight
Weight training						
Weight training						
Cool Down						

Class	Time	Calories

Notes	Total Time	Total Calories
	Rate Your Workout	Nailed it
		Spot on
		Average
		Meh
		OOOPS

Day:	Date:

Today I am grateful for:

My positive thought for the day is:

"Sweat is just fat crying."

Breakfast	Lunch
Dinner	Snacks

Water	1	2	3	4	5	6	7	8	9	10	11	12	13	14	15

Sleep Time	Supplements
Bed – _____	
Awake – _____	
Total – _____	

Rating	1	2	3	4	5

What will I make better tomorrow?

Name of Run:		
Start:	Stop:	Total:

Warm up				
Run		Time	Distance	Calories

Route

Weight training	Weight	Weight	Weight	Reps	Weight	Reps
	Reps	Reps	Reps	Reps	Reps	Reps
Weight training	Weight	Weight	Weight	Weight	Weight	Weight
	Reps	Reps	Reps	Reps	Reps	Reps
Cool Down						

Class	Time	Calories

Notes	Total Time	Total Calories
	Rate Your Workout	Nailed it
		Spot on
		Average
		Meh
		OOOPS

This Week's Goals

Factor	Current	Goal
Distance		
Weight		
Body Fat		
Other		

Workout	Nutrition

Other	Reward

Any new habits to develop?

Any old habits to ditch?

Day:	Date:

Today I am grateful for:

My positive thought for the day is:

"Exercise, my natural high."

Breakfast	Lunch

Dinner	Snacks

Water	1	2	3	4	5	6	7	8	9	10	11	12	13	14	15

Sleep Time	Supplements
Bed – _____	
Awake – _____	
Total – _____	

Rating	1	2	3	4	5

What will I make better tomorrow?

Name of Run:	

Start:	Stop:	Total:

		Time	Distance	Calories
Warm up				
Run				

Route

Weight training						
Weight training						
Cool Down						

Class	Time	Calories

Notes	Total Time	Total Calories
	Rate Your Workout	Nailed it	
		Spot on	
		Average	
		Meh	
		OOOPS	

Day:	Date:

Today I am grateful for:

My positive thought for the day is:

"You have to exercise, or at some point you'll just break down."

Breakfast	Lunch
Dinner	Snacks

Water	1	2	3	4	5	6	7	8	9	10	11	12	13	14	15

Sleep Time

      Bed – _____

      Awake – _____

      Total – _____

Supplements

Rating	1	2	3	4	5

What will I make better tomorrow?

Name of Run:		

Start:	Stop:	Total:

Warm up				

Run		Time	Distance	Calories

Route

Weight training		Weight	Weight	Weight	Weight	Weight	Weight
Weight training		Reps	Reps	Reps	Reps	Reps	Reps
Cool Down							

Class	Time	Calories

Notes	Total Time	Total Calories
	Rate Your Workout	Nailed it	
		Spot on	
		Average	
		Meh	
		OOOPS	

Day:	Date:

Today I am grateful for:

My positive thought for the day is:

"For food and exercise, while possessing opposite qualities, yet work together to produce health." Hippocrates

Breakfast	Lunch
Dinner	Snacks

Water	1	2	3	4	5	6	7	8	9	10	11	12	13	14	15

Sleep Time

    Bed – _____

    Awake – _____

    Total – _____

Supplements

Rating	1	2	3	4	5

What will I make better tomorrow?

Name of Run:		

Start:	Stop:	Total:

Warm up	

Run	Time	Distance	Calories

Route

Weight training						
Weight training						

Cool Down	

Class	Time	Calories

Notes	Total Time	Total Calories
	Rate Your Workout	Nailed it	
		Spot on	
		Average	
		Meh	
		OOOPS	

Day:	Date:

Today I am grateful for:

My positive thought for the day is:

"When it comes to health and well-being, regular exercise is about as close to a magic potion as you can get." Tich Nhat Hanh

Breakfast	Lunch
Dinner	Snacks

Water	1	2	3	4	5	6	7	8	9	10	11	12	13	14	15

Sleep Time

Bed – _____

Awake – _____

Total – _____

Supplements

Rating	1	2	3	4	5

What will I make better tomorrow?

Name of Run:						
Start:		Stop:		Total:		
Warm up						
Run		Time	Distance	Calories		
Route						
Weight training						
Weight training						
Cool Down						

Class	Time	Calories

Notes	Total Time	Total Calories
	Rate Your Workout	Nailed it
		Spot on
		Average
		Meh
		OOOPS

Day:	Date:

Today I am grateful for:

My positive thought for the day is:

"Running is not just exercise; it is a lifestyle." John Bingham

Breakfast	Lunch

Dinner	Snacks

Water	1	2	3	4	5	6	7	8	9	10	11	12	13	14	15

Sleep Time

Bed – _____

Awake – _____

Total – _____

Supplements

Rating	1	2	3	4	5

What will I make better tomorrow?

Name of Run:			
Start:	Stop:	Total:	

Warm up		
Run	Time	Distance	Calories

Route

Weight training						
Weight training						
Cool Down						

Class	Time	Calories

Notes	Total Time	Total Calories
	Rate Your Workout	Nailed it	
		Spot on	
		Average	
		Meh	
		OOOPS	

Day:	Date:

Today I am grateful for:

My positive thought for the day is:

"Once you are doing exercise regularly, the hardest thing is to stop it." Erin Gray

Breakfast	Lunch
Dinner	Snacks

Water	1	2	3	4	5	6	7	8	9	10	11	12	13	14	15

Sleep Time	Supplements
Bed – _____	
Awake – _____	
Total – _____	

Rating	1	2	3	4	5

What will I make better tomorrow?

Name of Run:		
Start:	Stop:	Total:

Warm up		
Run	Time	Distance	Calories

Route

Weight training						
Weight training						
Cool Down						

Class	Time	Calories

Notes	Total Time	Total Calories
	Rate Your Workout	Nailed it
		Spot on
		Average
		Meh
		OOOPS

Day:	Date:

Today I am grateful for:

My positive thought for the day is:

"If you don't make time for exercise, you'll probably have to make time for illness." Robin Sharma

Breakfast	Lunch

Dinner	Snacks

Water	1	2	3	4	5	6	7	8	9	10	11	12	13	14	15

Sleep Time	Supplements
Bed – _____	
Awake – _____	
Total – _____	

Rating	1	2	3	4	5

What will I make better tomorrow?

Name of Run:		
Start:	Stop:	Total:

Warm up				
Run		Time	Distance	Calories

Route

Weight training						
Weight training						
Cool Down						

Class	Time	Calories

Notes	Total Time	Total Calories
	Rate Your Workout	Nailed it
		Spot on
		Average
		Meh
		OOOPS

This Week's Goals

Factor	Current	Goal
Distance		
Weight		
Body Fat		
Other		

Workout	Nutrition

Other	Reward

Any new habits to develop?

Any old habits to ditch?

Day:	Date:

Today I am grateful for:

My positive thought for the day is:

"Take care of your body. It's the only place you have to live in."
Jim Rohn

Breakfast	Lunch
Dinner	**Snacks**

Water															

Sleep Time	Supplements
Bed – _____	
Awake – _____	
Total – _____	

Rating					

What will I make better tomorrow?

Name of Run:		
Start:	Stop:	Total:

Warm up	

Run	Time	Distance	Calories

Route

Weight training						
Weight training						

Cool Down	

Class	Time	Calories

Notes	Total Time	Total Calories
	Rate Your Workout	Nailed it
		Spot on
		Average
		Meh
		OOOPS

Day:	Date:

Today I am grateful for:

My positive thought for the day is:

"The doctor of the future will give no medicine but will involve the patient in the proper use of food, fresh air, and exercise." Thomas Edison

Breakfast	Lunch

Dinner	Snacks

Water	1	2	3	4	5	6	7	8	9	10	11	12	13	14	15

Sleep Time	Supplements
Bed – _____	
Awake – _____	
Total – _____	

Rating	1	2	3	4	5

What will I make better tomorrow?

Name of Run:		
Start:	Stop:	Total:

Warm up			
Run	Time	Distance	Calories

Route

Weight training						
Weight training						
Cool Down						

Class	Time	Calories

Notes	Total Time	Total Calories
	Rate Your Workout	Nailed it
		Spot on
		Average
		Meh
		OOOPS

Day:	Date:

Today I am grateful for:

My positive thought for the day is:

"Today I will love myself enough to exercise."

Breakfast	Lunch
Dinner	Snacks

Water	1	2	3	4	5	6	7	8	9	10	11	12	13	14	15

Sleep Time	Supplements
Bed – _____	
Awake – _____	
Total – _____	

Rating	1	2	3	4	5

What will I make better tomorrow?

Name of Run:				
Start:	Stop:		Total:	

Warm up				
Run		Time	Distance	Calories

Route

Weight training						
Weight training						
Cool Down						

Class	Time	Calories

Notes	Total Time	Total Calories	
	Rate Your Workout	Nailed it	
		Spot on	
		Average	
		Meh	
		OOOPS	

Day:	Date:

Today I am grateful for:

My positive thought for the day is:

"Walking is the best possible exercise. Habituate yourself to walk very far." Thomas Jefferson

Breakfast	Lunch
Dinner	Snacks

Water															

Sleep Time

    Bed – _____

    Awake – _____

    Total – _____

Supplements

Rating		2	3	4	5

What will I make better tomorrow?

Name of Run:			
Start:	Stop:		Total:

Warm up			
Run	Time	Distance	Calories

Route

Weight training						
Weight training						
Cool Down						

Class	Time	Calories

Notes	Total Time	Total Calories
	Rate Your Workout	Nailed it
		Spot on
		Average
		Meh
		OOOPS

Day:	Date:

Today I am grateful for:

My positive thought for the day is:

"Fitness starts in your head. You must choose to eat clean, exercise regularly, and treat your body with respect."

Breakfast	Lunch

Dinner	Snacks

Water	1	2	3	4	5	6	7	8	9	10	11	12	13	14	15

Sleep Time	Supplements
Bed – _____	
Awake – _____	
Total – _____	

Rating	1	2	3	4	5

What will I make better tomorrow?

Name of Run:		
Start:	Stop:	Total:

Warm up				
Run		Time	Distance	Calories

Route

Weight training		Weight	Reset	Weight	Weight	Weight	Weight
Weight training							
Cool Down							

Class	Time	Calories

Notes	Total Time	Total Calories
	Rate Your Workout	Nailed it
		Spot on
		Average
		Meh
		OOOPS

Day:	Date:

Today I am grateful for:

My positive thought for the day is:

"I'm addicted to exercising and I have to do something every day."
Arnold Schwarzenegger

Breakfast	Lunch
Dinner	Snacks

Water	1	2	3	4	5	6	7	8	9	10	11	12	13	14	15

Sleep Time	Supplements
Bed – _____	
Awake – _____	
Total – _____	

Rating	1	2	3	4	5

What will I make better tomorrow?

Name of Run:			
Start:	Stop:	Total:	

Warm up			
Run		Time	Distance	Calories

Route

Weight training		Reps	Weight	Reps	Weight	Reps	Weight
Weight training							
Cool Down							

Class	Time	Calories

Notes	Total Time	Total Calories
	Rate Your Workout	Nailed it	
		Spot on	
		Average	
		Meh	
		OOOPS	

Day:	Date:

Today I am grateful for:

My positive thought for the day is:

"Remember that any exercise is better than no exercise." Anonymous

Breakfast	Lunch
Dinner	Snacks

Water	1	2	3	4	5	6	7	8	9	10	11	12	13	14	15

Sleep Time	Supplements
Bed – _____	
Awake – _____	
Total – _____	

Rating	1	2	3	4	5

What will I make better tomorrow?

Name of Run:		
Start:	Stop:	Total:

Warm up				
Run		Time	Distance	Calories

Route

Weight training		Weight	Weight	Weight	Weight	Weight	Weight
Weight training		Weight	Weight	Weight	Weight	Weight	Weight
		lbs	lbs	lbs	lbs	lbs	lbs
Cool Down							

Class	Time	Calories

Notes	Total Time	Total Calories
	Rate Your Workout	Nailed it	
		Spot on	
		Average	
		Meh	
		OOOPS	

Conclusion

That's it. Ten weeks. Well Done.

Let's see how you've done.

	Start	End
Weight		
Body Fat %		
Neck		
Arm		
Chest		
Waist		
Hips		
Thigh		
Calf		

Like this journal? Scan the QR code below for other journals available.

www.chrisallton.co.uk/journals

Printed in Great Britain
by Amazon

57718335R00098